ANNABEL LEE

The poem: Edgar Allan Poe

The artist: Gilles Tibo

Tundra Books

Illustrations copyright © 1987 by Gilles Tibo

Published in Canada by Tundra Books, *McClelland & Stewart Young Readers,*
481 University Avenue, Toronto, Ontario M5G 2E9

Published in the United States by Tundra Books of Northern New York,
P.O. Box 1030, Plattsburgh, New York 12901

Library of Congress Catalog Number: 98-60313

Canadian Cataloguing in Publication Data

Poe, Edgar Allan, 1809-1849
   Annabel Lee: the poem

ISBN 0-88776-230-1

I. Tibo, Gilles, 1951- . II. Title.

PS2606.A1 1998   j811'.3   C98-930760-3

We acknowledge the support of the Canada Council for the Arts for our publishing program.

We acknowledge the financial support of the Government of Canada through the Book
Publishing Industry Development Program for our publishing activities.

Design by K. T. Njo

Printed and bound in Canada

1 2 3 4 5 6   03 02 01 00 99 98

To Bernard, my father, thank you

It was many and many a year ago,
In a kingdom by the sea

That a maiden there lived, whom you may know
By the name of Annabel Lee;

And this maiden she lived with no other thought
Than to love and be loved by me.

I was a child and *she* was a child,
In this kingdom by the sea,

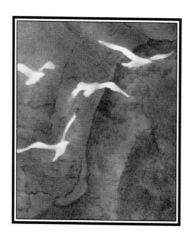

But we loved with a love that was more than love –
I and my Annabel Lee –
With a love that the winged seraphs of heaven
Coveted her and me.

And this was the reason that, long ago,
  In this kingdom by the sea,
A wind blew out of a cloud, chilling
  My beautiful Annabel Lee;

So that her highborn kinsmen came
    And bore her away from me,
To shut her up in a sepulcher
    In this kingdom by the sea.

The angels, not half so happy in heaven,
    Went envying her and me —
Yes! — that was the reason (as all men know,
    In this kingdom by the sea)
That the wind came out of the cloud by night,
    Chilling and killing my Annabel Lee.

But our love it was stronger by far than the love
 Of those who were older than we –
 Of many far wiser than we –
And neither the angels in heaven above,
 Nor the demons down under the sea,
Can ever dissever my soul from the soul
 Of the beautiful Annabel Lee:

For the moon never beams, without bringing me dreams
   Of the beautiful Annabel Lee;
And the stars never rise, but I feel the bright eyes
   Of the beautiful Annabel Lee:

And so, all the night-tide, I lie down by the side
Of my darling – my darling – my life and my bride,
  In the sepulcher there by the sea –
  In her tomb by the sounding sea.

335109